A Prayerbook for Couples

Cameron M. Thompson

&

Edited by

Rev. Nick VanDenBroeke

A Prayerbook for Couples

Copyright © 2017 Acropolis Scholars, LLC

ISBN: 0692872108
ISBN-13: 978-0692872109

DEDICATION

To all those men and women united in or
preparing for the great sacrament of holy
matrimony, may God continue to bless you
abundantly and help you with his grace to ever
more deeply participate in and show forth the love
and union between Christ and the Church.

CONTENTS

"Pray unceasingly."
1 Thessalonians 5:17

"For where two or three are gathered together
in my name, there I am in the midst of them."
Matthew 18:20

Forward

by Fr. Nick VanDenBroeke

Marriage and family life are the future of the Church and of the world. As Saint Pope John Paul II wrote, "*The future of humanity passes by way of the family.*" For this reason, after preaching the Gospel and celebrating the sacraments, marriage and family life is one of my highest priorities as a priest.

We can look at our culture and lament the disintegration of marriages and families, or we can look to the hope that we see in families that are united in Christ and flourishing in his love. In fact, there is great hope and encouragement I see in so many wonderful couples who have made the Lord the center of their lives.

Whenever I prepare a couple for marriage or meet with a couple for spiritual and pastoral counseling, I nearly always ask about their prayer life, both individually and as a couple, because a life of prayer must be the foundation of a marriage, and marriages thrive where prayer is central.

Of course, there is the saying: "The family that prays together, stays together". Well, one of the most stunning statistics about marriage confirms that this is absolutely true: the divorce rate for couples who pray together every day is less than 1%. And that alone should give couples the motivation to begin daily prayer together. This statistic shouldn't surprise us though, because if God is real (and he is), and if he loves us and wants to help couples love one another (and he does), then it makes perfect sense that the couple who prays together will receive the graces they need to live a happy and holy marriage.

This prayer book for married couples came about as a result of conversations Cameron Thompson and I have had about the importance of helping couples learn to pray, both individually and as a couple. We wanted to provide something simple and straightforward, but which will help couples begin a life of prayer together. My hope is that this booklet will give couples the encouragement they need to invite the Lord deeper into their marriage through prayer together as a couple.

May God bless you.

Father Nick VanDenBroeke

Introduction

Why pray together as a couple?

By the Sacrament of Matrimony, husband and wife are brought into union with one another through a sacramental mystery by which they share in and make present the union of Christ the Bridegroom and His Bride the Church. The Christian family is called the *ecclesia domestica*, the church of the home. In their marriage and in their parenting, husband and wife carry out in a special way their baptismal anointing as priest, prophet, and king in Christ. The Sacrament they share in confers on them the grace and duty to pray with and for one another with that same love that unites Christ the Bridegroom and the Church which is His Bride and Body.

"The Christian family is the first place of education in prayer. Based on the sacrament of marriage, the family is the "domestic church" where God's children learn to pray "as the Church" and to persevere in prayer. For young children in particular, daily family prayer is the first witness of the Church's living memory as awakened patiently by the Holy Spirit."[1]

Questions About Prayer

What is prayer?

"Prayer is the raising of one's mind and heart to God or the requesting of good things from God."[2]

The different kinds of prayer can generally be classified as *Worship & Adoration*, *Blessing*, *Petition & Intercession*, and *Prayer of the Heart*.

What is *Worship or Adoration*?

"Adoration is the first attitude of man acknowledging that he is a creature before his Creator. It exalts the greatness of the Lord who made us and the almighty power of the Savior who sets us free from evil."[3]

What is *Blessing*?

Everything we have is a blessing from the Lord. He blesses us and all his creation in many and varied ways, and in response to these gifts we bless and praise Him. "Blessing expresses the basic movement of Christian prayer: it is an encounter between God and man. In blessing, God's gift and man's acceptance of it are united in dialogue with each other. The prayer of blessing is man's response to God's gifts: because God blesses, the human heart can in return bless the One who is the source of every blessing."[4]

What is *Petition & Intercession*?

Petition is asking something from God, who is our loving Father. We can ask God for things because He has promised to provide for all our needs if we but ask Him. When we ask God for something on behalf of another person, that prayer is called 'intercession'.

"We are creatures who are not our own beginning, not the masters of adversity, not our own last end. We are sinners who as Christians know that we have turned away from our Father. Our petition is already a turning back to him."[5]

"When we share in God's saving love, we understand that every need can become the object of petition. Christ, who assumed all things in order to redeem all things, is glorified by what we ask the Father in his name."[6]

The first and greatest thing we can ask the Lord for is his Mercy. To ask of God to have mercy on us means to ask *both* that He forgive us for the sins we've committed *and* that He provide for all our needs, even before we know them. The word 'mercy' (*eleos/ eleison*) is the origin of the word 'alms'. We beg for alms from God, since we are poor in relation to Him, and He is rich in goodness and love. God grants all our needs in perfect love.

It is good to pray for specific people and needs. We should not be afraid to intercede for others specifically by name, which can be very powerful intercession.

What is *Prayer of the Heart*?

Prayer of the Heart is communion with God of heart being spoken to by heart. It is a prayer from within the core of one's being motivated by a love too deep for words. "For me, prayer is a surge of the heart; it is a simple look turned toward heaven…"[7]

What should we do physically when we pray?

Because human persons are both body and soul, we pray with our bodies as well as our words. Christianity has always had a tradition of certain postures and gestures associated with prayer. Some of these are probably familiar to you (**kneeling**, **genuflecting**, the **sign of the cross**). There are others as well which are worth mentioning: **standing with outstretched hands** (petition or thanksgiving), **bowing** (reverence), and **prostrations** (kneeling and then bowing one's head to the ground) which is a gesture of adoration and loving humility. Using these gestures and postures can be a means of deepening our prayer with greater conviction and sincerity, since it involves our whole being, and not only our words.

When should we pray?

The Bible exhorts us to pray always and without ceasing, so that everything we do becomes a prayer. We cannot pray at all times if we do not pray at specific times.[8] There are certain times throughout daily life (e.g. morning, at meals, evening, and night) that the people of God have traditionally dedicated specifically for prayer. The tradition of daily times of prayer goes back to time immemorial. One example of this is the *Liturgy of the Hours*. The Church prays the *Liturgy of the Hours* at set times throughout the day, which is a continuation of the practice of the Early Church, which itself grew out of the ancient worship of God in the Temple by the people of Israel.

Basic Prayers

The Apostle's Creed

"This synthesis of faith was not made to accord with human opinions, but rather what was of the greatest importance was gathered from all the Scriptures, to present the one teaching of the faith in its entirety. and just as the mustard seed contains a great number of branches in a tiny grain, so too this summary of faith encompassed in a few words the whole knowledge of the true religion contained in the Old and the New Testaments."[9] *"This Creed is the spiritual seal, our heart's meditation and an ever-present guardian; it is, unquestionably, the treasure of our soul."*[10]

The Apostle's Creed

I believe in God, the Father Almighty, Creator of Heaven and earth;

And in Jesus Christ, His only Son Our Lord, Who was conceived by the Holy Spirit, born of the Virgin Mary, suffered under Pontius Pilate, was crucified, died, and was buried.

He descended into Hell; the third day He rose again from the dead; He ascended into Heaven, and is seated at the right hand of God, the Father almighty; from there He will come to judge the living and the dead.

I believe in the Holy Spirit, the holy Catholic Church, the communion of saints, the forgiveness of sins, the resurrection of the body and life everlasting.

Amen.

The Our Father

*The **Lord's Prayer** (The "**Our Father**") is the summary of the whole Gospel.[11] "The Lord's Prayer is the most perfect of prayers. In it we ask, not only for all the things we can rightly desire, but also in the sequence that they should be desired. This prayer not only teaches us to ask for things, but also in what order we should desire them."[12] Praying the Lord's Prayer, we join Christ's eternal prayer to the Father; we are sons and daughters of God, praying to our God and Father that His will (perfect love) be done and His kingdom (eternal joy) come, that He sustain us, forgive us, and protect us from all that is harmful.*

Our Father, Who art in heaven, hallowed be Thy name; Thy kingdom come; Thy will be done on earth as it is in heaven. Give us this day our daily bread; and forgive us our trespasses as we forgive those who trespass against us; and lead us not into temptation, but deliver us from evil. Amen.

The Hail Mary

*The **Hail Mary** is the Salutation to Mary, the new Eve: Mother of all the Living. It begins with the words of the Gospel, and concludes by asking her intercession. Prayer to Mary the Mother of God has been a deep part of Christian Life from the very beginning of the Church.*

Hail Mary, full of grace. The Lord is with thee. Blessed art thou among women, and blessed is the fruit of thy womb, Jesus. Holy Mary, Mother of God, pray for us sinners, now and at the hour of our death, Amen.

The Glory Be

*The "**Glory be**" is a prayer of exaltation of the Holy Trinity, and an affirmation of His eternal perfection the same in the beginning, today, and unto ages of ages.*

Glory be to the Father, and to the Son, and to the Holy Spirit, as it was in the beginning, is now, and ever shall be, world without end. Amen.

The Rosary

The Rosary is a longer prayer that is made up of a number of these three prayers. The Rosary is organized into five "decades" of **1 Our Father, 10 Hail Mary's, 1 Glory be** each, usually signified by beads. On each of these five decades, we meditate on a mystery from the life of Christ.[13]

Prayers at Particular Times of Day

Morning Prayer

You are encouraged to pray the whole of Morning Prayer when time allows. When time is short, you may pray any portion of it. Make the sign of the Cross whenever you see the '✝' symbol.

The prayer is structured for each spouse to have a particular role: one spouse can lead the prayer (Leader), and the other can read the petitions (Reader). You can alternate roles as you choose. Two options for the psalm are listed here, feel free to pray either one or both of them.

Opening

Leader: ✝ God, come to my assistance,

Reader: Lord, make haste to help me.

Either **from Psalm 148**

L: Praise the LORD from the heavens; praise him in the heights.

R: Praise him, all his angels; praise him, all his hosts.

L: Praise him, sun and moon; praise him, all shining stars.

R: Praise him, highest heavens, and the waters above the heavens.

L: Let them praise the name of the LORD. He commanded: they were created.

R: He established them forever and ever, gave a law which shall not pass away.

Together: Glory be to the Father, and to the Son, and to the Holy Spirit, as it was in the beginning, is now, and ever shall be, world without end. Amen.

Or

from Psalm 103

L: My soul, give thanks to the Lord.
All my being, bless his holy name.

R: My soul, give thanks to the Lord
and never forget all his blessings.

L: It is he who forgives all your guilt,
who heals every one of your ills,

R: who redeems your life from the grave, who crowns you with love and compassion.

Together: Glory be…

Prayers of Petition

R: For the peace from above and the salvation of our souls, let us pray to the Lord.

Together: Lord, have mercy.

R: That this whole day may be perfect, holy, peaceful, and sinless, let us pray to the Lord.

Together: Lord, have mercy.

R: For good weather, an abundance of the fruits of the earth, and peaceful times, let us pray to the Lord.

Together: Lord, have mercy.

R: For all our family, that the Lord will grant us health, happiness, perfect love, and provide for all our needs, let us pray to the Lord.

Together: Lord, have mercy.

Together: Our Father…

Morning Offering & Closing Prayer

L: Heavenly Father, through the priesthood of Christ given to us at our baptism, we offer to you all that we do today. May all our actions, O Lord, begin with your inspiration and carry on with your help, so that our prayer and work may always begin with you and through you reach completion. We ask this through our Lord Jesus Christ your Son, who lives and reigns with you and the Holy Spirit, one God, forever and ever.

Together: Amen.

L: + May the Lord bless us, protect us from all evil and bring us to everlasting life.

Together: Amen.

Night Prayer

The lighting of a lamp or candle during night prayer goes back to the earliest days of the Church, and even to the ancient worship in the temple of Jerusalem. The words of this part of the prayer are taken from the Gospel of John (about the creation of the world) and the Book of Revelation (about the eternal world to come).

You are encouraged to pray the whole of Night Prayer when time allows. When time is short, you may pray any portion of it.

Opening Prayer and Lighting of the Lamp

Together: + In the name of the Father, and of the Son, and of the Holy Spirit.

Leader *(lighting the lamp/candle)***:** In the beginning was the Word, and the Word was with God, and the Word was God. He was in the beginning with God; all things were made through him, and without him was not anything made that was made. In him was life, and the life was the light of men. The light shines in the darkness, and the darkness has not overcome it. *(John 1:1-5)*

Reader: And when He comes again, the night shall be no more; they will need no light from lamp or sun, for the Lord God will be their light, and they shall reign for ages of ages. Amen. *(Rev. 22:5)*

Prayers of Repentance and Forgiveness

Together: I confess to almighty God, and to you, my brothers and sisters, that I have greatly sinned in my thoughts and in my words, in what I have done and what I have failed to do, through my fault, through my fault, through my most grievous fault; therefore I ask the blessed Mary ever-virgin, all the angels and saints, and you my brothers and sisters, to pray for me to the Lord our God.

Together: May almighty God have mercy on us, forgive us our sins, and bring us to everlasting life. Amen.

Together: Lord, have mercy.
Christ, have mercy.
Lord, have mercy.

Psalm and Collect

Together: May my prayer arise before you like incense, O Lord, and the raising of my hands like an evening oblation. *(Psalm 141:2)*

Leader: Let us Pray.

Together: Visit this house, we beg you, O Lord, and drive far from it all snares of the enemy. May your holy angels dwell here to keep us in peace, and may your blessing be upon us always, through Christ our Lord. Amen.

Night Offering and Closing Prayer

Leader: Thank you, Lord, for this day and bringing us to this night; we offer you this past day, and all that we are and all that we have, and we commend ourselves to your care; accept us as a pleasing oblation through Christ, with Him, and in Him, O God, almighty

Father, in the unity of the Holy Spirit, to whom be all honor and glory forever. Amen.

Reader: + May the Lord bless us, protect us from all evil and bring us to everlasting life.

Together: Amen.

Blessing Before Meals

(traditional prayer)

> **Leader:** The eyes of all hope in You, O Lord,

> **Reader:** and You give them their food at the proper time.

> **Together:** + Bless us, O Lord, and these Thy gifts which we are about to receive from Thy bounty, through Christ our Lord. Amen.

Thanksgiving After Meals

(traditional prayer)

> **Leader:** You open wide your hand, O Lord,

> **Reader:** And grant the desires of every living thing.

> **Together:** + We give you thanks, almighty God, for all Your benefits: Who live and reign for ever and ever.

Short Litany of Petition and Intercession

This litany of petitions is prayed at any time of day, and asks God for his mercy and blessings. You may add your own personal petitions and intercessions at the end.

Together: Lord, Have Mercy.
Christ, Have Mercy.
Lord, Have Mercy.

Leader: Blessed are you, God of our Fathers,

Response: praiseworthy and glorious forever.

L: + Let us bless the Father, and the Son, with the Holy Spirit.

R: Let us praise and exalt Him above all forever.

L: Blessed are you, O Lord, in the firmament of heaven.

R: praiseworthy and glorious and exalted above all forever

L: May the all-powerful and merciful Lord bless and keep us all the days of our life.

R: Amen.

L: Grant, O Lord, to preserve us from sin

R: all throughout this day/night

L: Have Mercy on us, O Lord

R: Have Mercy on us

L: May your mercy be upon us always, O Lord,

R: for we have hoped in you

L: O Lord, hear my prayer

R: And let my cry come unto you.

Together: Our Father…

Prayer Commemorating the Incarnation of Christ
(the *Angelus*)

The Angelus is an ancient prayer commemorating the Incarnation of Jesus as a sign of God's infinite love for us, and has been traditionally prayed at 6am, 12pm, and 6pm.

Leader: The Angel of the Lord declared unto Mary,
Response: and she conceived by the Holy Spirit.
Together: Hail Mary…

Leader: Behold, the handmaid of the Lord,
Response: let it be done unto me according to your word.
Together: Hail Mary…

Leader: And the Word became flesh
Response: and dwelt among us.
Together: Hail Mary…

Leader: Pray for us, O Holy Mother of God,
Response: That we may be made worthy of the promises of Christ.

Together: Let us Pray. Pour forth, we beseech, thee, O Lord, thy grace into our hearts, that we to whom the Incarnation of Christ thy son was made known by the message of an angel, may by his passion and cross be brought to the glory of his resurrection through the same Christ, our Lord. Amen.

Other Short Prayers

The Marriage Prayer of Tobias
(Tobit 8:5-8)

This prayer comes from The Book of Tobit in the Old Testament. After each enduring much suffering and hardship, in both of their families, Tobias is led by Archangel Raphael to Sarah who is to be his wife. Tobias and Sarah fall deeply in love and find salvation in the grace of God through their marriage. On their wedding night, they kneel down in prayer and offer this praise to God which recalls the origin of marriage from the beginning of creation, and begs God in simplicity for lasting love between husband and wife and that He deliver them from harm and provide for all their needs.

Leader: Let us pray that the Lord may have mercy on us.

Together: Blessed are you, O God of our fathers, and blessed be your holy and glorious name for ever. Let the heavens and all your creatures bless you. You made Adam out of the dust of the earth and gave him Eve his wife as a helper and support, and from them the whole race of mankind has sprung. You said, 'It is not good that the man should be alone; let us make a helper for him like himself.'

Husband: And now, O Lord, I am not taking this wife of mine because of lust, but with sincerity.

Wife: Grant that we may find mercy and grow old together.

Together: Amen.

Prayer Asking Mary's Help

(the *Memorare*)

Mary is the first human person made entirely sanctified by God through union with her son, Jesus Christ. Christians have always sought her help and prayers as our mother who sits in heaven, body and soul in union with Jesus our Lord.

Remember, O most gracious Virgin Mary, that never was it known that anyone who fled to thy protection, implored thy help, or sought thy intercession, was left unaided. Inspired with this confidence, we fly to thee, O Virgin of virgins, our Mother. To thee we come, before thee we stand, sinful and sorrowful. O Mother of the Word Incarnate, despise not our petitions, but in thy clemency, hear and answer us. Amen.

Prayer in Distress

(*Sub Tuum Praesidium*)

Leader: + God, come to my assistance.
Response: Lord, make haste to help me.

Together: We fly under thy protection for refuge, Holy Mother of God; despise not our petitions in our needs, but from all dangers deliver us always, O Glorious and Blessed Virgin.

Prayer for Deliverance from Evil

Leader: + God, come to my assistance.
Response: Lord, make haste to help me.

Together: Let God arise, and let His enemies be scattered. Let them that hate Him flee from before His Face. + Behold the cross of the Lord. Flee from here, you powers of the enemy!

Prayer of Thanksgiving

Alleluia! Praise God in His sanctuary, praise Him in His mighty firmament. Praise Him for His powerful deeds; praise Him for His boundless grandeur. O praise Him with sound of trumpet; praise Him with lute and harp. Praise Him with timbrel and dance; praise Him with strings and pipes. O praise Him with resounding cymbals; praise Him with clashing of cymbals. Let everything that breathes praise the Lord! Alleluia! (*Psalm 150*)

Prayer for the Dead
(an Ancient Prayer of the Church)

> **Leader:** Eternal rest grant unto him/her/them, O Lord,
> **Response:** And Let perpetual light shine upon him/her/them.
> **Leader:** May he/she/they rest in peace. Amen.

> **Together:** Out of the depths I cry to you, O Lord; Lord, hear my voice! O let your ears be attentive to the voice of my pleadings! If you, O Lord, should mark iniquities, Lord, who could stand? But with you is found forgiveness, that you may be revered. I long for you, O Lord, my soul longs for his word. My soul hopes in the Lord more than the watchman for daybreak. More than watchmen for daybreak, let Israel hope in the Lord. For with the Lord there is mercy, and with him plenteous redemption. It is he who will redeem Israel from all its iniquities. *(Psalm 130)*

Vows & Prayers from the Wedding Mass

Vows

The bridegroom says: I, _____, take you, _____, to be my wife. I promise to be faithful to you in good times and in bad, in sickness and in health, to love you and to honor you all the days of my life.

The bride says: I, _____, take you, _____, to be my husband. I promise to be faithful to you in good times and in bad, in sickness and in health, to love you and to honor you all the days of my life.

Nuptial Blessing of the Couple

O God, who by your mighty power created all things out of nothing, and, when you had set in place the beginnings of the universe, formed man and woman in your own image, making the woman an inseparable helpmate to the man, that they might no longer be two, but one flesh, and taught that what you were pleased to make one must never be divided;

O God, who consecrated the bond of Marriage by so great a mystery that in the wedding covenant you foreshadowed the Sacrament of Christ and his Church;

O God, by whom woman is joined to man and the companionship they had in the beginning is endowed with the one blessing not forfeited by original sin nor washed away by the flood.

Look now with favor on these your servants, joined together in Marriage, who ask to be strengthened by your blessing. Send down on them the grace of the Holy Spirit and pour your love into their hearts, that they may remain faithful in the Marriage covenant.

May the grace of love and peace abide in your daughter _____, and let her always follow the example of those holy women whose praises are sung in the Scriptures. May her husband entrust his heart to her, so that, acknowledging her as his equal and his joint heir to the life of grace, he may show her due honor and cherish her always with the love that Christ has for his Church.

And now, Lord, we implore you: may these your servants hold fast to the faith and keep your commandments; made one in the flesh, may they be blameless in all they do; and with the strength that comes from the Gospel, may they bear true witness to Christ before all; may they be blessed with children, and prove themselves virtuous parents, who live to see their children's children. And grant that, reaching at last together the fullness of years for which they hope, they may come to the life of the blessed in the Kingdom of Heaven. Through Christ our Lord.

Preface

It is truly right and just, our duty and our salvation, always and everywhere to give you thanks, Lord, holy Father, almighty and eternal God, through Christ our Lord.

For in him you have made a new covenant with your people, so that, as you have redeemed man and woman by the mystery of Christ's Death and Resurrection, so in Christ you might make them partakers of divine nature and joint heirs with him of heavenly glory.

In the union of husband and wife you give a sign of Christ's loving gift of grace, so that the Sacrament we celebrate might draw us back more deeply into the wondrous design of your love.

And so, with the Angels and all the Saints, we praise you, and without end we acclaim: Holy, Holy, Holy, Lord God of hosts…

Meditations on the Sacrament of Married Life

Reflection on the relationship of husband and wife

When you two are united to one another in the Sacrament of Matrimony, you become the sacrament of Christ's union with His bride the Church, made present in the world, and in your consecrated union, you become the sacrament of Christ's love for one another. This means that in your day to day life, you are living God's passionate love for one another and can become the living sign of his mercy for one another through the living out of your mutual love and affection.

Paul's letter to the Ephesians reveals that in the living out of the Sacrament of Matrimony the husband reveals the nature of Christ the Head and Bridegroom and the wife reveals the nature of the Christ's Bride and Body the

Church. This means that when you look at your spouse, you should strive to see the presence of Christ in your spouse, and your spouse in Christ. There is a mystical way in which you are the image of Christ for one another.

Reflection on life with Children

When you have children and baptize them into the Church, you are not only raising sons and daughters for yourselves, but also increasing the number of the sons and daughters of God. The growth of your family is the growth of the whole Church and thus the extension of Christ's visible presence in the world.

Christ has promised us in the Gospels (Matthew 25:40) that "whatsoever you do for the least of mine, you've done unto me," and "whoever receives one such child in my name receives me." This means that whatsoever you do for one another and for your children, you do so also for Christ. In this way, you will live out in your family the reality of God's overflowing love for the whole world.

Prayer for your Marriage

Almighty and Eternal Father, as you created man and woman for one another from the beginning, and have made the union of husband and wife the very sacrament and sign of Christ's union with the Church — your very love for humanity, we ask you to bless us in our life together that we may fall ever more passionately in love with one another and with you, and be more perfectly the sacrament of your mercy and love for one another.   Grant that we may ever more deeply participate in and manifest, through our marriage, the mystery of your love incarnate in Jesus Christ. Grant that we may enjoy together a peaceful life on this earth and be together in union with you and one another for all eternity in your heavenly kingdom, where Christ reigns in union with you and the Holy Spirit, God for ever and ever. Amen.

Notes

[1] *CCC* 2685
[2] *CCC* 2590
[3] *CCC* 2628
[4] *CCC* 2626
[5] *CCC* 2629
[6] *CCC* 2633
[7] *CCC* 2558
[8] *CCC* 2697
[9] *CCC* 186
[10] *CCC* 197
[11] *CCC* 2761
[12] *CCC* 2763
[13] For a list of these mysteries, see Appendix A.

Appendix A:
Mysteries of the Rosary

The Joyful Mysteries

1. The Annunciation to Mary and Incarnation of Jesus

2. Mary visits her cousin Elizabeth

3. The Nativity of Jesus

4. Jesus is presented in the Temple

5. Finding the child Jesus in the Temple after searching for three days

The Sorrowful Mysteries

1. Christ's agony in the garden of Gethsemane

2. Jesus is whipped at the pillar

3. Jesus Christ is crowned with thorns

4. Jesus carries his cross

5. Jesus is crucified and dies on the cross

The Luminous Mysteries

1. Christ is baptized by John in the River Jordan
2. Christ turns water into wine at the Wedding in Cana
3. The Proclamation of the Kingdom of God
4. Christ is transfigured on Mount Tabor and his divinity shines forth
5. Jesus institutes the Eucharist at the Last Supper

The Glorious Mysteries

1. Jesus Christ rises from the dead
2. Jesus ascends into Heaven
3. The Holy Spirit descends upon the disciples at Pentecost
4. Mary is taken body and soul into Heaven
5. Mary is crowned Queen of Heaven

Appendix B:
Further Reading on Prayer

Bunge, Gabriel. *Earthen Vessels: The Practice of Personal Prayer According to the Patristic Tradition*. San Francisco: Ignatius Press, 2002.

Catechism of the Catholic Church. Vatican City: Libreria Editrice Vaticana, 2000.

Dubay, Thomas. *Prayer Primer: Igniting a Fire Within*. San Francisco, CA: Ignatius Press, 2002.

Dubay, Thomas. *Deep Conversion, Deep Prayer*. San Francisco, CA: Ignatius Press, 2006.

Kreeft, Peter. *Prayer for Beginners*. San Francisco: Ignatius Press, 2000.